The TAO Of
TRAUMA HEALING

WORKBOOK

Dr. Christy Walter

Copyright © 2026 Dr. Christy Walter

All rights reserved.

The content contained within this book may not be reproduced, duplicated, or transmitted without direct written permission from the author or the publisher.

ISBN 978-1-964143-21-7

Published by Suncoast Digital Press, Inc.

Contents

Introduction

To fulfill my vision of helping people who struggle with anxiety, depression, and trauma, I developed and wrote *The TAO of Trauma Healing: A Proven Guide to Overcoming Anxiety & Depression*—"TAO" (from Chinese philosophy) meaning "the way" and "harmony with nature." I think of TAO as describing my unique approach in moving you "**T**hrough **A**nd **O**ut" of past trauma. My book intertwines my professional experiences as an emergency medicine physician and former psychotherapist with my own personal journey and the latest research.

The lessons in the book harness the power of neuroplasticity to produce lasting change and healing. The method is unique. I developed it and tested it on myself and others. Differing from other therapeutic modalities, my method is direct, bold, fast, and effective. *The TAO of Trauma Healing Workbook* is a complementary guide meant to be used in conjunction with the book. In a stepwise fashion, each lesson builds upon the one before. Each is meant to improve skills and resilience in small, doable action steps. The action steps can be implemented from day one.

This program changes lives. Your life can be changed, too. The tools gained by working through these lessons can improve your quality of life, offer lasting change, and lead to the way out of despair. The TAO of Trauma Healing is the way to hope, healing, happiness, and freedom.

About the Author

Dr. Christy Walter is a board-certified Emergency Medicine physician, former psychotherapist, author, speaker, life coach, and international health and healing advocate. She currently practices medicine as a traveling ER doctor, providing care to patients in underserved and understaffed areas of the country. She has a passion for horses, is active in her church, and spends time with her family and friends. She calls San Diego, CA home.

She can be reached through her Facebook page: The TAO of Trauma Healing.

Reflection & Writing Exercises for Lessons 1–12

Use this workbook alongside the main book. After each lesson, respond to the prompts below. Take your time, write large, and give yourself grace as you go.

Lesson 1 – Finding Freedom

Summary & Reflections:

In this lesson, I shared some of the feelings I experienced during my battle with depression, anxiety, and PTSD. Depression felt like a never-ending darkness where I was gripped by indecision, inability to concentrate, a lack of energy, hopelessness, and being unable to enjoy anything for more than a minute. I barely made it through each day. I thought of death constantly and even attempted suicide. Anxiety manifested as constant worry, a racing of the mind, difficulty in sleeping, catastrophizing, and symptoms associated with PTSD (disturbing flashbacks, panic, and rumination about what happened).

I was stuck in an endless cycle of despair. I knew something had to change. There were four messages I took to heart that helped me pivot:

1. Life is the sum total of what you are willing to accept.
2. I decided to decide that suicide was not an option and that I would do whatever it took to get better.
3. Acceptance.
4. God wants me to do something new.

I admitted that my life was the sum total of what I was willing to accept. With ending my life no longer an option, I accepted that I have a mental illness, an actual condition that needed to be proactively managed.

Ready to try something new, I started to incorporate affirmations and art into each and every day. The healing and positive outcomes were so profound that I was compelled to share my journey and methods to help others.

Prompts for Writing & Reflection

Use the space after each prompt to write your honest responses.

Prompt 1:   **Do you struggle with anxiety and/or depression? Explain.**

Prompt 2:   **What was your reaction to the statement, "Your life is the sum total of what you are willing to accept"?**

Prompt 3:   Are you content with your life the way it is now? If not, what do you want to change?

____

____

____

____

Prompt 4:   What words do you use to describe yourself?

____

____

____

____

Prompt 5:   Can you accept compliments? Why or why not?

____

____

____

____

Prompt 6:   Are you willing to do whatever it takes to change your life? Why or why not?

____

____

____

____

Prompt 7:   **Are you ready for change?**

Prompt 8:   **What do you think about the idea that you have the power to change your brain?**

Prompt 9:   **Do you do the same things expecting different results? Explain.**

Prompt 10:   **Are you willing to try something new? Why or why not?**

Coloring is an activity that is proven to soothe the mind and spirit. Set aside 20-60 minutes each day to devote to coloring. Play soft meditation music (something without lyrics to avoid distraction). You can use any coloring tool for this assignment. For example, I like to use colored pencils, while others enjoy crayons, markers, or charcoal. You can make as manycopies as you like of Happy Dog and give him a different look at each coloring session, or use other coloring book pages that appeal to you. The point of this exercise is to help your mind settle and focus, allow your body to relax, release endorphins and oxytocin (feel-good chemicals) into your brain, and to dip yourself into the creative part of your mind. I believe that we have been made in the image of God, our Creator. Tapping into and expressing your creativity is a spirit-connecting activity. Life gets busy, so do yourself a favor and mark the time you'd like to be coloring each day.

Keep the appointment—it's with a VIP!

Coloring Page: Happy Dog

Lesson 2 – Digging Out

Summary & Reflections:

This lesson focused on managing emotional dysregulation with practical, easy-to-implement tools, including a brain download and intention-setting exercise, boxed breathing, and optional spiritual exercise.

Prompts for Writing & Reflection

Use the space after each prompt to write your honest responses.

Prompt 1:　　Write it out: I recommend starting each day with this exercise. After you get up, get your morning coffee, etc., take out a piece of paper, notebook or journal and start your timer. Write for two minutes. Don't think about what you are writing, just write. Stop when you hit two minutes, regardless of where you're at. If two minutes is too long, then do one minute, but don't go any longer than two, so as not to flip into overwhelm.

____

____

____

____

____

____

____

____

____

____

Prompt 2:　　Reset: Now reset your mind. Instead of feelings and thoughts that are disempowering or upsetting, what would you prefer to bring to your day? It might be clarity, motivation, gratitude, calmness, or something else. Make this your intention for the day and note it on your paper.

____

____

____

____

Prompt 3:   Have you ever had a panic attack that interfered with your ability to work? Explain.

\
\
\
\

Prompt 4:   What techniques, if any, have you tried using to manage your anxiety in the past?

\
\
\
\
\

Prompt 5:   Do you worry about having a panic attack in the middle of the day? If so, how does the impact of this affect your life?

\
\
\
\

Prompt 6:   Did you perform the brain download and breathing exercises? If not, what prevented you from doing so? If you did the exercises, explain your responses to them.

\
\
\
\
\

Prompt 7:   Did you implement the brain download and/or breathing exercises when you felt uncomfortable feelings during the day? Explain.

Prompt 8:   Have you ever practiced, or do you practice any other meditative exercises? If so, what have you tried and how did you react to it?

Prompt 9:   Were you able to include any spiritual practices? If so, what did you include? If not, what got in the way/why didn't you include it?

Prompt 10:   Did you spend time trying the art exercise?

Prompt 11:   What was your overall experience of this week's lesson?

Coloring Page – Dig It

Lesson 3 – Rule Of 8's

Summary & Reflections:

1. You can walk out these steps by remembering The Rule of 8's:
   - Prioritize your sleep: 8 hours every night.
   - Drink your water: Eight 8-ounce glasses per day.
   - Eat your fruit and veggies: 8 servings per day.
   - Exercise your body: 8 minutes more activity each day.
2. Continue with the writing practice of the brain download, setting up your intention, and performing the boxed breathing technique from Lesson 2.
3. The art component for this lesson can be done as part of a meditative exercise with relaxing music. The process of doing art itself releases feel- good chemicals like oxytocin and activates the calming parasympathetic nervous system. This week's dog portrait is *Pooped Out Pug*.

Use this space to reflect on your experience practicing the Rule of 8's (sleep, water, food, movement, and daily habits). Congratulations! You are well on your way to freedom. Give yourself credit for coming this far!

____

____

____

____

____

____

____

____

____

____

____

____

____

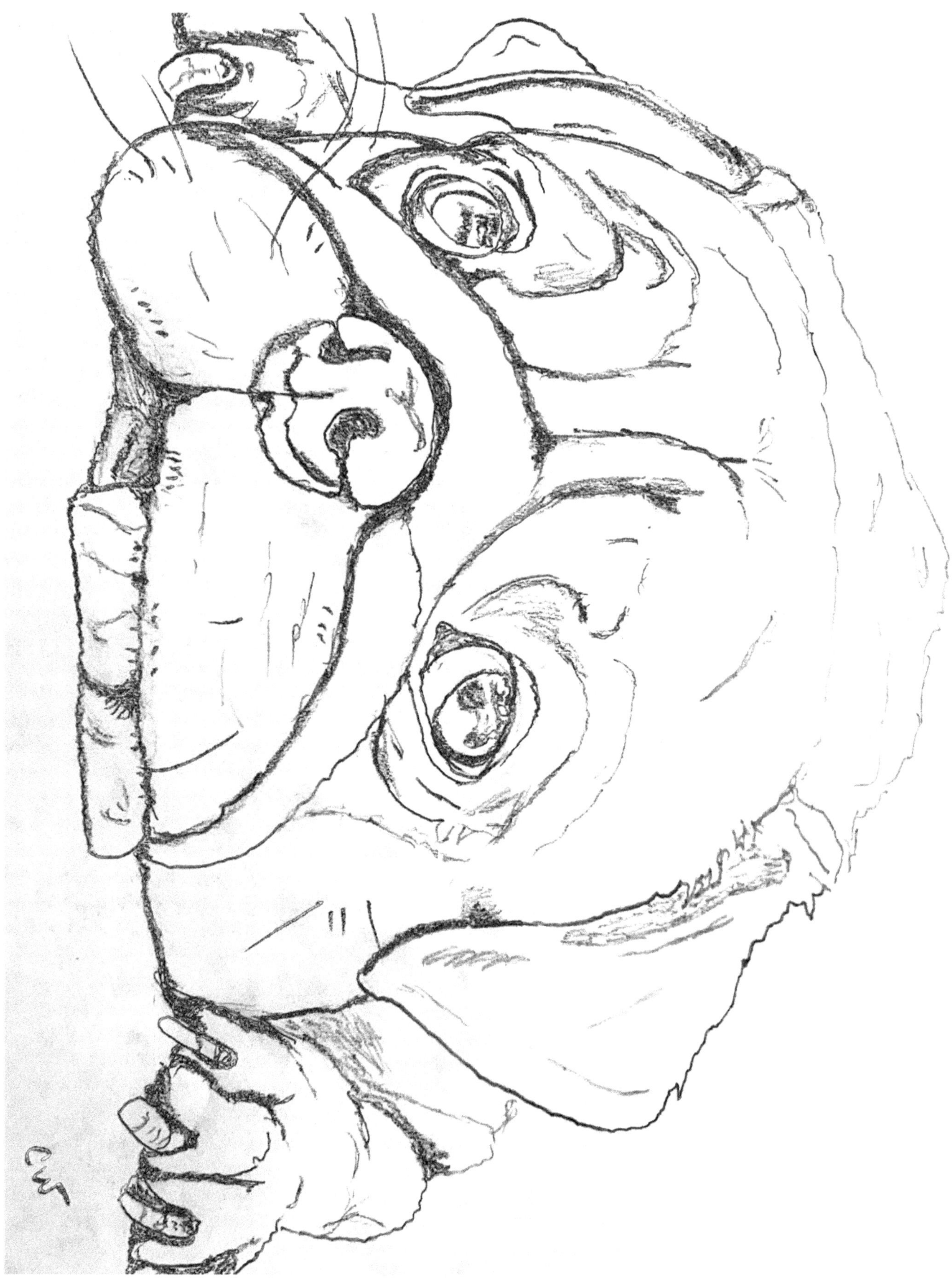

Coloring Page – Pooped Out Pug

Lesson 4 – As A Man Thinks

Summary & Reflections:

In this lesson, we learned that our core beliefs influence the way we think, which in turn influences our thoughts and actions. Our actions subsequently influence how we interact in the world around us and how we treat ourselves within it.

Repeated actions end up becoming habits. Then, the feedback we receive from our actions, whether positive or negative, reinforces our beliefs. To shift this self- defeating cycle, we reviewed action steps that combine spoken affirmations with actions you can implement to support the process of rewiring your brain into a healthier mindset.

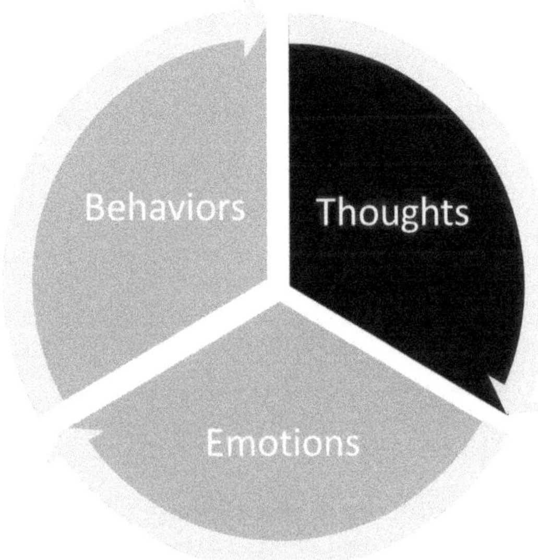

There are various techniques for identifying thought distortions that can change how you feel and think. For example, you may find yourself making "all-or-nothing" statements about your spouse, such as, "He always slams the door," or "She never understands me." Such all-or-nothing statements are considered distortions because typically, nothing is always or never true. Such extreme thinking undoubtedly affects your feelings about the other person and how you behave when you are around them.

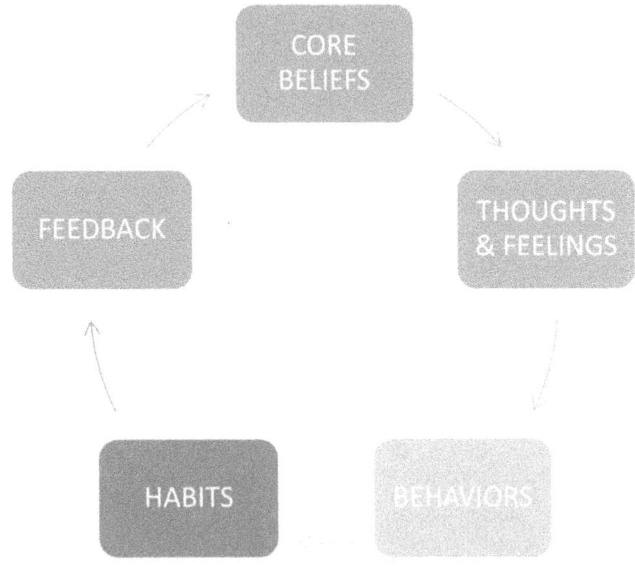

Prompts for Writing & Reflection

Use the space after each prompt to write your honest responses.

Prompt 1A: Make a list of 10 or more positive things about yourself. Ask your friends and family for ideas if needed. After you create your list read it out loud to yourself and envision yourself being it. Read these affirmations to yourself daily.

____

____

____

____

____

____

____

____

____

____

Prompt 1 B: How many positive affirmations were you able to come up with?

____

____

Prompt 2: Choose one affirmation to act on. For example, if one of your affirmations is, "I am generous," then practice being generous. Write down the affirmation you are going to act on.

____

____

____

Prompt 3: Were you able to identify any of your core beliefs? Explain.

____

____

____

Prompt 4: Explain how your core beliefs influence the way you think and feel.

Prompt 5: What behaviors or habits would you like to improve to be more positive and empowering? Write them down, even if right now you don't see when or how you could address them.

Prompt 6: What do you allow into your brain? For example, what do you watch on social media and television? What kinds of conversations do you engage in with your friends, coworkers, and family?

Prompt 7: Looking at the above and keeping in mind "GIGO," are there any "input" sources you are allowing that you'd characterize as, maybe not "garbage," but certainly not self- and life-affirming? What do you see as being counterproductive to your intention to uplift your mental and emotional health?

Coloring Page – Little Engine

Lesson 5 – Lions and Tigers and Bears

Summary & Reflections:

In this lesson, we discussed the body's response to stress. We looked at how the fight-or-flight response can be overused, leading to depleted energy stores. We explored how to identify and stop people, places, and things from robbing you of your energy, and we reviewed practical things you can do to restore your mind and body.

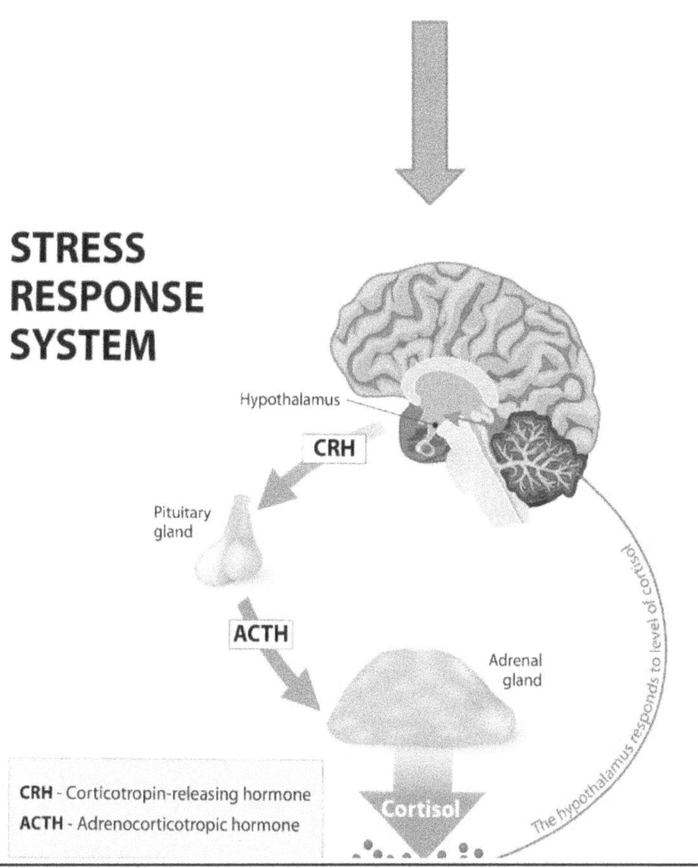

Relative Depletion of Cortisol

Prompts for Writing & Reflection

Use the space after each prompt to write your honest responses.

Prompt 1:   Name the top three energy drains in your life.

____

____

____

Prompt 2: **What do you currently do to refill your tank?**

____

____

____

____

____

____

____

____

____

____

Prompt 3: **Are there people in your life who demand a lot of your time and energy, but don't reciprocate?**

____

____

____

____

____

____

____

____

____

Additional Exercise – Energy Drains List

In your workbook or journal, start a list describing the behavior of a person or people who are chronic energy drains in your life.

____

____

____

____

____

____

____

____

____

Additional Exercise – Driver's Seat Affirmations

In The Tao of Trauma Healing Workbook or your journal, write three affirming statements about how you are in the driver's seat of your own life.

____

____

____

____

____

____

____

____

____

Coloring Page – Jack

Lesson 6 – Feeding Your Spirit

Summary & Reflections:

In this lesson, we discussed how to engage your five senses and how to use them to connect with nature, along with methods to use to calm down your mind. We identified the importance of feeding your spirit by connecting with something much bigger than yourself—in this case, nature. And we tied it into a grounding exercise where you activate your senses to bring yourself into the *now*.

Prompts for Writing & Reflection

Use the space after each prompt to write your honest responses.

Prompt 1:　　Did you do the exercise in this lesson? If not, what kept you from doing it? But if you did do it, what was the back-to-nature experience like for you?

____

____

____

____

____

Prompt 2:　　What senses were the easiest/ hardest for you to engage? Can you identify any situations that occurred recently where this practice could have helped you regulate your emotions?

____

____

____

____

Prompt 3:　　Being in the now can be challenging. Do you have a hard time letting go of the past?

____

____

____

____

Prompt 4:   Do you worry about the future? Explain.

____

____

____

____

____

Prompt 5:   Were you able to absorb the vastness of nature during this exercise?

____

____

____

____

____

Prompt 6:   Did you find anything that gave you a sense of awe?

____

____

____

____

Prompt 7:   What other ways do you or can you imagine would feed your spirit?

____

____

____

____

Coloring Page – Aspen

Lesson 7 – Self-Love

Summary & Reflections:

In this lesson, we discussed the fact that life is meant to be lived and enjoyed, not merely survived. We discovered pitfalls that can leave us feeling exhausted and empty, and discovered that finding the "true you" requires you to start with self-love. Self-love exercises included giving yourself permission to dial back the intensity, putting forth only 80% effort on any given day; practicing saying "no" and doing only what works for you; using soothing touch to comfort and calm yourself, and practicing self-forgiveness. To assist in self-forgiveness, we created a mantra to repeat as many times as needed until you are comfortable enough to accept the forgiveness. We learned that it is okay to honor yourself and that you are "right on time."

Prompts for Writing & Reflection

Use the space after each prompt to write your honest responses.

Prompt 1: **Do less. No more than 80% effort. You don't have to be a super mom, top producer, selfless volunteer, or the sounding board for everyone else's problems. In fact, you need to do just the opposite.**

____

____

____

____

____

____

____

Prompt 2: **Were you able to let go of 20% of the things you would normally do, to reach the 80% goal? If so, what did you decide to leave off your schedule? If not, why was it difficult to let things go?**

____

____

____

____

____

____

____

Prompt 3: By freeing up your time, were you able to carve out space for self- discovery? Write what comes to mind when you ask yourself who you really are.

____

____

____

____

____

Prompt 4: When did you catch yourself before over-promising and said "no" instead? Did you find it hard to say "no"?

____

____

____

____

____

Prompt 5: Were you able to use soothing touch to calm yourself when upset? Were you able to be gentle with yourself and also to allow yourself to feel comforted? Explain.

____

____

____

____

____

Prompt 6: Write about the practice of self-forgiveness. Did you try the mantra outlined in the lesson? Did it feel awkward? Was it easy? Were you able to take it in? What did you unload off your back that you'd been carrying from the past? Do you feel lighter?

____

____

____

____

____

Coloring Page – Amara ('I Love Me' dog portrait)

Lesson 8 – Values and Vision

Summary & Reflections:

In this lesson, we discovered the importance of identifying your core values and how those values provide a window into your authentic self. Those values also provide an internal compass from which to operate. Identifying and operating within those values brings clarity, direction, and contentment. Living outside of what you truly value brings nothing more but confusion, isolation, exhaustion, and defeat. The action steps for this lesson are to complete the following values exercise, describe your future successful self on a vision board or in writing, and then make your actions match those values.

Values and Graph Exercise

1. You will see a table with 3 vertical columns and 20 horizontal rows. In column 1 there is a list of 80 words group in a series of 4 words per row. Start this exercise by going to the first row of words. You will notice there are 4 words in this row. From this row choose the one word that best resonates with you and write your answer in the first space in column 2. Next, go to the second row of words and choose the word that resonates with you and write that down in the second space in column 2. Continue this for each group of 4. Once you reach the last row you will have identified the top 20 words that represent your values.

2. Now that you have completed the first step you will have 20 words written down in column 2. Now narrow those 20 words down to 10. You do this by comparing pairs of words in column 2. The pairs include 1 & 2, 3 & 4, 5 & 6, 7 & 8, 9 & 10, 11 & 12, 13 & 14, 15 & 16, 17 & 18, 19 & 20. From each pair you will again write down the word that resonates with you in column 3. Once you reach the last pair of words you will have identified the top 10 words that represent your values.

3. From the final 10 words remaining in column 3, circle your top 5 choices. These are your core values.

Column 1	Column 2	Column 3
Acceptance, Accountability, Achievement, Attitude	1.	1.
Authenticity, Balance, Boldness, Character	2.	
Collaboration, Commitment, Compassion, Competence	3.	2
Confidence, Contentment, Courage, Creativity	4.	

Dedication, Dependability, Devotion, Discipline	5.	3
Discovery, Diversity, Efficiency, Empathy	6.	
Encouragement, Endurance, Enthusiasm, Excellence	7.	4.
Fairness, Family, Fitness, Generosity	8.	
Gentleness, Goodness, Growth, Honesty	9.	5
Honor, Hope, Humility, Humor	10.	
Independence, Integrity, Intimacy, Joy	11.	6
Justice, Kindness, Leadership, Learning	12.	

Love, Loyalty, Obedience, Openness	13.	7
Order, Passion, Patience, Peace	14.	
Perseverance, Personal Growth, Quality, Relationships	15.	8.
Reliability, Respect, Sacrifice, Security	16.	
Self-Control, Self-Discipline, Selflessness, Simplicity	17.	9.
Spirituality, Steadfast, Submission, Teachable	18.	
Teamwork, Thankfulness, Tranquility, Transparency	19.	10.
Trustworthiness, Truth, Unity, Wisdom	20.	

Prompts for Writing & Reflection

Use the space after each prompt to write your honest responses.

Prompt 1: Describe your future successful self, either through creating a vision board or by writing a paragraph or two. Gaining some clarity on your values and what you hold important will be a springboard you can use to come up with ideas. Be as detailed as possible. Include what you look like, what you are doing, how you feel, and what relationships you want in your future. Don't worry if it seems impossible. Imagine what you would be like if you weren't dealing with anxiety and depression. Let your imagination go wild. If you can imagine it, you can create it.

____

____

____

____

____

____

____

Prompt 2: Picture your values and successful self in your mind. Do your actions match? Focus on your actions being congruent with your values.
For example, if you value freedom and debt is keeping you from experiencing freedom, then plan how you will curb your spending and eliminate your debt.
If you value spirituality, then build in some daily practices that honor your spirituality. If you value family, then think of how you can spend more time interacting with them.
Values clarity comes from your authentic self and makes all decision-making much easier. Life is more peaceful and enjoyable.

____

____

____

____

____

____

____

Prompt 3: Have you tried to live up to what you think other people expect of you? If so, how does it feel?

Prompt 4: List your top five values.

Prompt 5: When you were narrowing down your choices, did you find yourself wanting to answer what you thought you "should" answer? Explain.

Coloring Page – Inari ('successful one' dog portrait)

Lesson 9 – The Trauma Brain

Summary & Reflections:

In this lesson, we acknowledged that we all have experienced trauma at some point. We reviewed various kinds of traumatic experiences. These included acute, chronic, complex, historical, secondary, and vicarious traumas. We further discussed brain anatomy and how the brain processes trauma. We also learned that unprocessed trauma could leave you responding to conflict and other perceived dangers in unhealthy ways.

Dorsolateral Pre-Frontal Cortex - Rational Brain

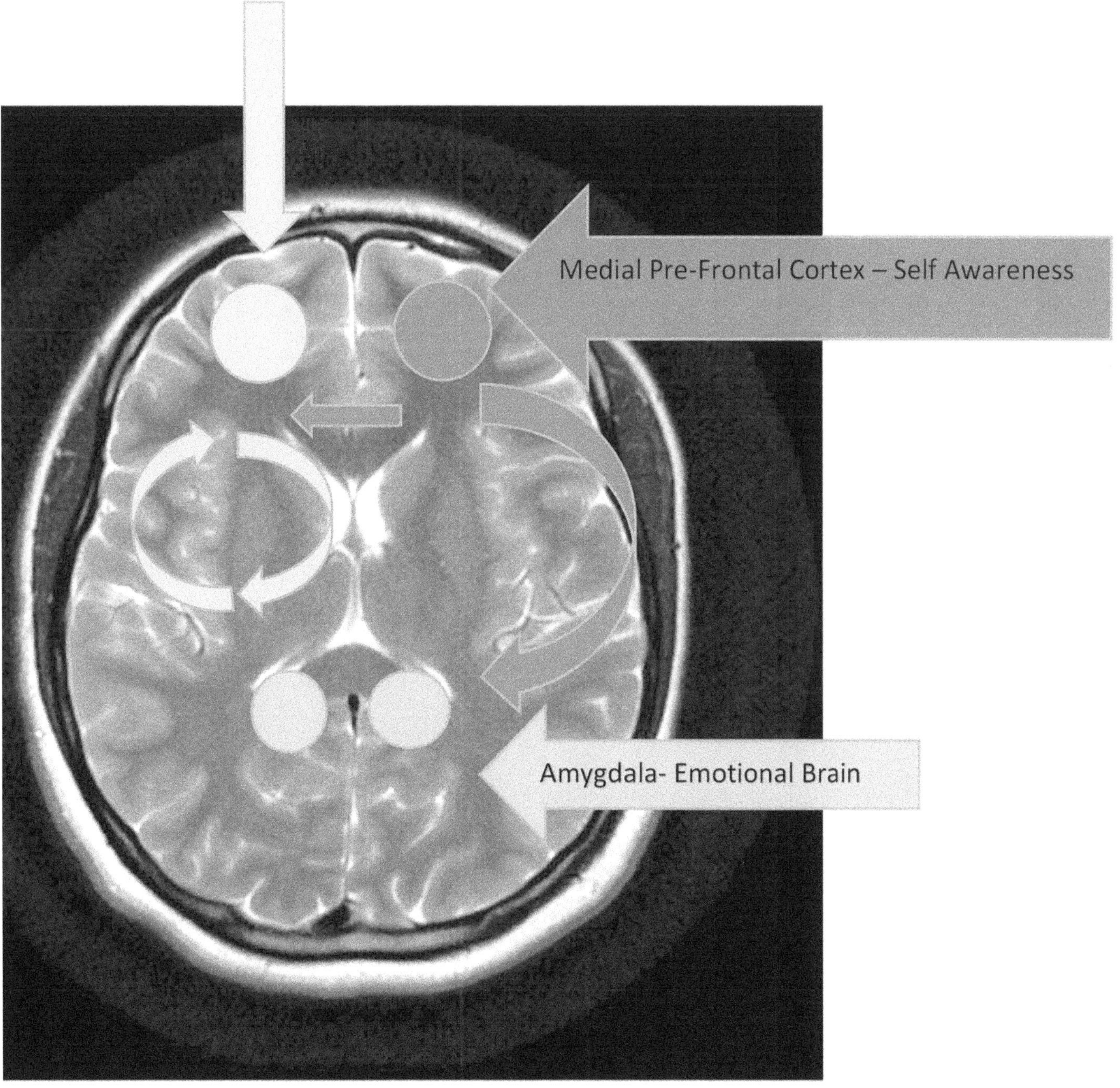

Trauma Jar Exercise

Imagine an empty jar. Inside the jar, you will add (draw) large marbles—each marble represents one past trauma.

As you add the marbles give each a label with a word or short phrase for each trauma you can recall.

Don't overthink it; this is just a starting point.

Prompts for Writing & Reflection

Use the space after each prompt to write your honest responses.

Prompt 1: **Fight, flight, freeze, or fawn? Write down examples of ways you have responded to stressors, danger, conflict, or trauma in the past and present.**

____

____

____

____

____

Prompt 2:   Were you able to identify the different types of trauma (acute, chronic, secondary, etc.) in your life? Explain.

____

____

____

____

Prompt 3:   Do you think that traumatic experiences from your past affect your life now? Explain.

____

____

____

____

Prompt 4:   And are there any activities, places, objects, or people in your life currently that bring up thoughts, images, or feelings from past trauma?

____

____

____

____

Prompt 5:   What do you usually do when you are triggered?

____

____

____

____

Prompt 6:   How many marbles did you draw in your trauma jar? Were there more or fewer than you would have guessed?

____

____

____

____

Coloring Page – Phoebe

Lesson 10 – The TAO of Trauma Healing

Summary & Reflections:

In this lesson, we learned that whether you experience "big T trauma(s) or "little t" trauma(s), it impacts your mind (thoughts, will, and emotions), as well as the physical brain and the body itself. Left unprocessed, the trauma you have experienced can continue to dominate your life and leave you stuck in the past. We discussed some forms of therapy that therapists use to help their clients to move past trauma. This lesson guided us through a process that I developed that involves (1) facing the trauma, (2) tracing the feelings associated with the trauma, (3) embracing the impact of the trauma on your life, (4) erasing the effects of the trauma, and finally, 5) replacing the trauma with a new template of truth. This is called the Tao of Trauma Healing method.

Step 1 – Face the trauma

Identify and write down one trauma you will work on with the TAO method this week.

Trauma I am choosing to work on:

____

____

____

____

Step 2 – Trace the trauma

Do a brain download (free writing) about this trauma. Write whatever comes to mind for about two minutes, using the lines below.

After you write, choose a single feeling word to describe how you feel. Write it down and repeat the brain download process. Then identify the next feeling word. From the new feeling word, do another brain download. Continue this process until you reach a neutral, or less charged feeling. I recommend spending no more than 30 minutes on this step. You can pick it up again on a different day. Once you reach a neutral feeling you can move onto step 3.

____

____

____

____

____

____

____

____

Feeling word 1:

____

Feeling word 2:

____

Feeling word 3:

____

Feeling word 4:

____

____

If you have not reached a neutral feeling continue this process on a separate sheet of paper. Repeat until you reach a neutral feeling or until you reach 30 minutes, whichever comes first.

____

____

____

____

Step 3 – Embrace the trauma

Write in first person ("I…") about how this trauma has affected your life. Include any ways it has impacted you in these areas:

- Relationships
- Self-esteem and identity
- Career, school, or finances
- Health and habits
- Hopes, dreams, and your sense of the future

____

____

____

____

____

Step 4 – Erase the trauma-caused lies

Write down the lies you have believed as a result of this trauma (about yourself, other people, your relationships, or your future).

____

____

____

____

____

____

Step 5 – Replace the lies with truth

Using your affirmations (Lesson 4), core values (Lesson 8), and God's view of you, rewrite each lie as a life-giving truth.

____

____

____

____

____

You may also write statements to your younger self here (for example, "Little _____, you are worthy. Little _____, you are God's masterpiece.").

____

____

____

____

____

____

Reflection Questions for Lesson 10

After working through the TAO steps for one trauma, use these questions to reflect on your experience.

Prompt 1: **You have completed processing through your first trauma. How did it go? Did you reach a neutral emotional state? Or do you need to continue working through the process?**

____

____

____

____

____

____

Prompt 2:   What are 2-3 of the most damaging lies you've believed, as a result of your trauma?

____

____

____

____

____

____

____

Prompt 3:   Name a belief, habit, or behavior that you developed as a result of the trauma you've experienced.

____

____

____

____

____

____

Prompt 4:   What marble from your trauma jar will you choose to work on next?

____

____

____

____

____

____

____

Coloring Page – Hank

Lesson 11 – The Power of Community

Summary & Reflections:

In this lesson, we explored the idea that we all desire and need connection— connection with our Creator and connection with others. Connection through a relationship with the Lord fills our spirit and strengthens our connection with our authentic self. Building friendships with others can nurture your soul as well. We discussed the health benefits (both physically and mentally) of being part of a meaningful community—community where you can be loved and accepted just the way you are.

Prompts for Writing & Reflection

Use the space after each prompt to write your honest responses.

Prompt 1:   **How would you describe your relationship with God? How do you nurture that relationship? What could you do to strengthen it?**

Prompt 2:   **Write about your closest friend. How do they make you feel supported? Encouraged?**

Prompt 3: What do you think they value most about their friendship with you?

Prompt 4: Are you satisfied with your circle of friends? Why or why not?

Prompt 5: What is one thing you can do to expand your community of support? What would be the best possible outcome for you if you did that?

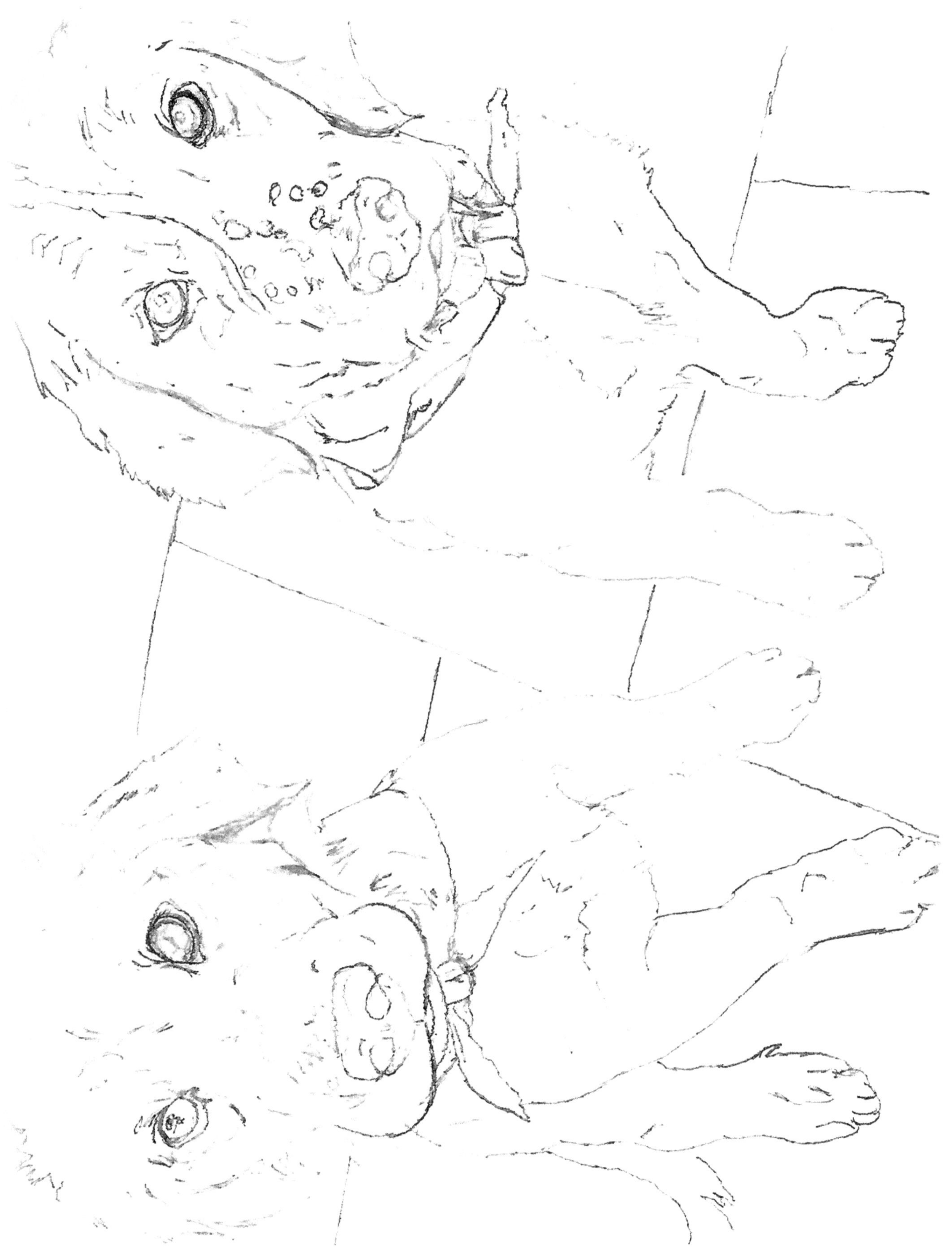

Coloring Page – Friends Forever

Lesson 12 – Gratitude

Summary & Reflections:

In this lesson, we learned that our brains gravitate toward negativity and that it takes five positive encounters to offset one negative encounter. We learned that there are many physical and mental health benefits to practicing gratitude. Gratitude requires intentional effort, and it takes practice to master it. Several methods were discussed for you to use to practice gratitude.

Prompts for Writing & Reflection

Use the space after each prompt to write your honest responses.

Prompt 1: Buddy walks of gratitude: You know that person who you perhaps decided to buddy up with for a morning walk every week? As well as improving your mood by enjoying this social connection and healthy activity, agree to spend 5 minutes during the walk taking turns expressing gratitude. Example: "I'm grateful for my granddaughter calling me just to say hello." (Other person takes a turn.) "I'm grateful that my knee feels good enough today for me to walk with you." Then it's your turn, and so on.

Prompt 2:   Is this glass half-empty or half-full? If you see the glass as half-full, congratulations. You are practicing gratitude. Explain the benefits of this perspective. If you see the glass as half-empty, you are not alone. Write about how it might feel if you saw the glass as half-full.

____

____

____

____

____

____

____

Prompt 3:   Shifting your perspective requires intention. Name a struggle in your life and describe how you can shift your perspective about it. What would it look like if you reframed it as a gift rather than a hardship?

____

____

____

____

____

____

____

Prompt 4:   List three things you are grateful for and explain why.

____

____

____

____

____

Prompt 5: Of the suggestions presented in this lesson, which tool will you use to intentionally practice gratitude?

Prompt 6: If you didn't find a tool you liked, write down what you are willing to try.

Coloring Page – Snoopy

www.ingramcontent.com/pod-product-compliance
Lightning Source LLC
Chambersburg PA
CBHW042009070726

47599CB00043B/2037